50 Mac and Cheese Dishes for the House

By: Kelly Johnson

Table of Contents

- Classic Baked Mac and Cheese
- Lobster Mac and Cheese
- Bacon Jalapeño Mac and Cheese
- Truffle Mac and Cheese
- Buffalo Chicken Mac and Cheese
- Four Cheese Mac and Cheese
- BBQ Pulled Pork Mac and Cheese
- Spinach and Artichoke Mac and Cheese
- Vegan Mac and Cheese
- Chili Mac and Cheese
- Crab Mac and Cheese
- Jalapeño Popper Mac and Cheese
- Greek Mac and Cheese with Feta
- Mushroom and Thyme Mac and Cheese
- Buffalo Cauliflower Mac and Cheese
- Cajun Mac and Cheese
- Bacon and Tomato Mac and Cheese

- Sweet Potato Mac and Cheese
- Broccoli Cheddar Mac and Cheese
- Mac and Cheese with Caramelized Onions
- Pesto Mac and Cheese
- Cauliflower Mac and Cheese
- Mac and Cheese with Sausage
- Baked Mac and Cheese with Breadcrumbs
- Four Meat Mac and Cheese
- Mac and Cheese with Roasted Red Peppers
- Mediterranean Mac and Cheese
- Blue Cheese and Walnut Mac and Cheese
- Truffle Oil and Mushroom Mac and Cheese
- Mac and Cheese with Ham and Peas
- BBQ Chicken Mac and Cheese
- Mac and Cheese with Spinach and Bacon
- Smoked Gouda Mac and Cheese
- Mac and Cheese with Roasted Garlic
- Lobster and Spinach Mac and Cheese
- Mac and Cheese with Sundried Tomatoes

- Mac and Cheese with Chorizo
- Buffalo Ranch Mac and Cheese
- Mac and Cheese with Caramelized Shallots
- Mac and Cheese with Crispy Onions
- Mac and Cheese with Roasted Brussels Sprouts
- Mac and Cheese with Ham and Mustard
- Mac and Cheese with Sriracha
- Mac and Cheese with Prosciutto
- Mac and Cheese with Spinach and Artichokes
- Mac and Cheese with Chives and Bacon
- Mac and Cheese with Gorgonzola
- Mac and Cheese with Smoked Salmon
- Mac and Cheese with Roasted Butternut Squash
- Mac and Cheese with Pulled Beef

Classic Baked Mac and Cheese

Ingredients:

- 1 lb elbow macaroni
- 4 cups sharp cheddar cheese, shredded
- 2 cups milk (whole)
- 1/4 cup unsalted butter
- 1/4 cup all-purpose flour
- 1 tsp Dijon mustard (optional)
- Salt and pepper to taste
- 1 cup breadcrumbs (optional, for topping)

Instructions:

1. Cook macaroni according to package until al dente, drain and set aside.
2. In a saucepan, melt butter over medium heat. Whisk in flour to form a roux, cook 2 minutes.
3. Gradually whisk in milk, cook until thickened (5–7 minutes).
4. Remove from heat, stir in mustard, salt, pepper, and 3 cups cheese until melted.
5. Mix cheese sauce with macaroni. Pour into a greased baking dish.
6. Top with remaining cheese and breadcrumbs (if using).
7. Bake at 350°F (175°C) for 25-30 minutes until bubbly and golden.

Lobster Mac and Cheese

Ingredients:

- Classic Mac and Cheese base (see above)
- 1 lb cooked lobster meat, chopped
- 1/2 cup Gruyère cheese, shredded
- 1 tbsp lemon juice
- 1 tbsp chives, chopped

Instructions:

1. Prepare classic mac and cheese sauce, stirring in Gruyère along with cheddar.
2. Fold lobster meat and lemon juice into macaroni and cheese sauce.
3. Bake as per classic recipe, sprinkle chives on top before serving.

Bacon Jalapeño Mac and Cheese

Ingredients:

- Classic Mac and Cheese base
- 6 slices cooked bacon, crumbled
- 2 jalapeños, seeded and diced
- 1 cup pepper jack cheese, shredded

Instructions:

1. Prepare classic sauce, mix in pepper jack cheese.
2. Fold in bacon and jalapeños with macaroni.
3. Bake as usual, garnish with extra jalapeño slices or bacon if desired.

Truffle Mac and Cheese

Ingredients:

- Classic Mac and Cheese base
- 2 tbsp truffle oil or 1 tsp truffle salt
- 1/2 cup Parmesan cheese, shredded
- Fresh parsley, chopped (for garnish)

Instructions:

1. Prepare classic cheese sauce, stir in Parmesan and truffle oil/salt.
2. Combine with macaroni and bake.
3. Garnish with parsley.

Buffalo Chicken Mac and Cheese

Ingredients:

- Classic Mac and Cheese base
- 2 cups cooked shredded chicken
- 1/2 cup buffalo sauce (adjust to taste)
- 1/2 cup blue cheese crumbles
- 1 cup mozzarella cheese

Instructions:

1. Toss shredded chicken with buffalo sauce.
2. Prepare cheese sauce (mix cheddar and mozzarella).
3. Combine macaroni, cheese sauce, and buffalo chicken.
4. Bake and sprinkle blue cheese crumbles on top before serving.

Four Cheese Mac and Cheese

Ingredients:

- Classic Mac and Cheese base
- 1 cup sharp cheddar
- 1 cup Gruyère
- 1/2 cup mozzarella
- 1/2 cup Parmesan

Instructions:

1. Melt butter, whisk flour, add milk to make roux.
2. Stir in all four cheeses until melted and smooth.
3. Combine with cooked macaroni and bake.

BBQ Pulled Pork Mac and Cheese

Ingredients:

- Classic Mac and Cheese base
- 2 cups cooked pulled pork
- 1/2 cup BBQ sauce
- 1 cup smoked gouda cheese, shredded

Instructions:

1. Mix pulled pork with BBQ sauce.
2. Prepare cheese sauce with cheddar and gouda.
3. Combine macaroni, cheese sauce, and pulled pork.
4. Bake and optionally top with extra pulled pork.

Spinach and Artichoke Mac and Cheese

Ingredients:

- Classic Mac and Cheese base
- 1 cup cooked chopped spinach (squeeze out excess water)
- 1 cup chopped marinated artichoke hearts
- 1/2 cup cream cheese
- 1/2 cup mozzarella cheese

Instructions:

1. Stir cream cheese and mozzarella into cheese sauce.
2. Fold in spinach and artichokes with macaroni.
3. Bake until bubbly.

Vegan Mac and Cheese

Ingredients:

- 1 lb elbow macaroni (or gluten-free if preferred)
- 1 1/2 cups raw cashews (soaked in hot water for 30 min)
- 1 cup unsweetened almond milk (or other plant milk)
- 1/4 cup nutritional yeast
- 2 tbsp lemon juice
- 1 tsp garlic powder
- 1 tsp onion powder
- 1 tsp smoked paprika
- Salt and pepper to taste
- 2 tbsp olive oil or vegan butter
- 1/4 cup breadcrumbs (optional)

Instructions:

1. Cook macaroni and set aside.
2. Drain cashews and blend with almond milk, nutritional yeast, lemon juice, garlic powder, onion powder, smoked paprika, salt, and pepper until very smooth.
3. Heat olive oil in a pan, add sauce and warm gently.
4. Combine sauce with pasta and pour into baking dish.
5. Top with breadcrumbs if desired and bake at 350°F for 20 minutes until golden.

Chili Mac and Cheese

Ingredients:

- Classic mac and cheese base (see previous classic recipe)
- 1 cup cooked chili (beef or vegetarian)
- 1 cup cheddar cheese
- 1/2 cup diced tomatoes (canned or fresh)
- 1/4 cup diced onions
- 1 tsp chili powder

Instructions:

1. Prepare classic cheese sauce, add chili powder.
2. Fold chili, tomatoes, onions, and cheese sauce with macaroni.
3. Bake at 350°F for 25 minutes until bubbly.

Crab Mac and Cheese

Ingredients:

- Classic mac and cheese base
- 1 lb lump crab meat (fresh or canned, drained)
- 1/2 cup Old Bay seasoning
- 1/2 cup shredded Gruyère cheese
- 1 tbsp fresh parsley, chopped

Instructions:

1. Prepare cheese sauce with cheddar and Gruyère.
2. Fold crab meat, Old Bay seasoning, and parsley into macaroni and cheese.
3. Bake for 25 minutes at 350°F.

Jalapeño Popper Mac and Cheese

Ingredients:

- Classic mac and cheese base
- 3 jalapeños, diced (seeds removed for less heat)
- 1 cup cream cheese
- 1 cup shredded cheddar cheese
- 1/2 cup cooked and crumbled bacon (optional)
- 1/4 cup panko breadcrumbs

Instructions:

1. Mix cream cheese and cheddar into the classic cheese sauce.
2. Stir in jalapeños and bacon with macaroni.
3. Bake and top with breadcrumbs.

Greek Mac and Cheese with Feta

Ingredients:

- Classic mac and cheese base
- 1 cup crumbled feta cheese
- 1/2 cup chopped kalamata olives
- 1/2 cup sun-dried tomatoes, chopped
- 1 tbsp fresh oregano or thyme

Instructions:

1. Prepare cheese sauce, stir in feta.
2. Mix olives, sun-dried tomatoes, and oregano with macaroni and cheese sauce.
3. Bake until hot and bubbly.

Mushroom and Thyme Mac and Cheese

Ingredients:

- Classic mac and cheese base
- 2 cups mixed mushrooms (shiitake, cremini, button), sliced
- 2 tbsp butter
- 2 cloves garlic, minced
- 1 tsp fresh thyme leaves
- 1 cup Gruyère cheese

Instructions:

1. Sauté mushrooms and garlic in butter until tender.
2. Prepare cheese sauce with cheddar and Gruyère.
3. Stir mushrooms and thyme into macaroni and cheese.
4. Bake as usual.

Buffalo Cauliflower Mac and Cheese

Ingredients:

- Classic mac and cheese base
- 2 cups roasted cauliflower florets tossed in buffalo sauce
- 1/2 cup blue cheese crumbles
- 1 cup shredded cheddar cheese
- 1/2 cup mozzarella cheese

Instructions:

1. Toss cauliflower in buffalo sauce and roast at 425°F for 20 minutes.
2. Prepare cheese sauce with cheddar and mozzarella.
3. Fold roasted cauliflower into mac and cheese.
4. Bake and top with blue cheese crumbles.

Cajun Mac and Cheese

Ingredients:

- Classic mac and cheese base
- 1 tbsp Cajun seasoning
- 1 cup smoked sausage, sliced
- 1/2 cup diced bell peppers (red and green)
- 1/2 cup diced onions
- 1 cup pepper jack cheese

Instructions:

1. Sauté sausage, peppers, and onions with Cajun seasoning until cooked.
2. Prepare cheese sauce with cheddar and pepper jack.
3. Combine everything with macaroni.
4. Bake at 350°F for 25 minutes.

Bacon and Tomato Mac and Cheese

Ingredients:

- 1 lb elbow macaroni
- 4 slices bacon, chopped
- 2 cups sharp cheddar cheese, shredded
- 1 cup milk
- 2 tbsp butter
- 2 tbsp flour
- 1 cup cherry tomatoes, halved
- Salt and pepper to taste

Instructions:

1. Cook macaroni according to package, drain.
2. In a skillet, cook bacon until crispy, remove and set aside.
3. In the same skillet, melt butter, whisk in flour, cook 1-2 minutes.
4. Slowly whisk in milk, cook until thickened.
5. Stir in cheddar cheese until melted.
6. Combine cheese sauce, macaroni, bacon, and tomatoes.
7. Bake at 350°F for 20 minutes if desired.

Sweet Potato Mac and Cheese

Ingredients:

- 1 lb elbow macaroni
- 1 large sweet potato, peeled and cubed
- 2 cups cheddar cheese
- 1 cup milk
- 2 tbsp butter
- 2 tbsp flour
- Salt, pepper, and nutmeg to taste

Instructions:

1. Boil sweet potato until tender, then mash until smooth.
2. Cook macaroni and drain.
3. Make roux with butter and flour, add milk and whisk until thickened.
4. Stir in cheese and mashed sweet potato until combined.
5. Mix with macaroni and bake at 350°F for 20 minutes.

Broccoli Cheddar Mac and Cheese

Ingredients:

- 1 lb elbow macaroni
- 2 cups broccoli florets, steamed
- 2 cups sharp cheddar cheese
- 1 cup milk
- 2 tbsp butter
- 2 tbsp flour
- Salt and pepper

Instructions:

1. Cook macaroni and steam broccoli until tender.
2. Prepare cheese sauce with butter, flour, milk, and cheddar.
3. Stir broccoli into macaroni and cheese sauce.
4. Bake at 350°F for 20 minutes if desired.

Mac and Cheese with Caramelized Onions

Ingredients:

- 1 lb elbow macaroni
- 2 large onions, thinly sliced
- 2 tbsp butter
- 2 cups cheddar cheese
- 1 cup milk
- 2 tbsp flour
- Salt and pepper

Instructions:

1. Cook macaroni.
2. Caramelize onions in butter on low heat for 30 minutes until golden.
3. Make cheese sauce with butter, flour, milk, and cheese.
4. Mix macaroni, cheese sauce, and caramelized onions.
5. Bake at 350°F for 20 minutes.

Pesto Mac and Cheese

Ingredients:

- 1 lb elbow macaroni
- 1 cup basil pesto
- 2 cups mozzarella cheese
- 1 cup Parmesan cheese
- 1 cup milk
- 2 tbsp butter
- 2 tbsp flour
- Salt and pepper

Instructions:

1. Cook macaroni.
2. Prepare cheese sauce with butter, flour, milk, mozzarella, and Parmesan.
3. Stir pesto into cheese sauce and mix with macaroni.
4. Bake at 350°F for 20 minutes.

Cauliflower Mac and Cheese

Ingredients:

- 1 lb elbow macaroni
- 2 cups cauliflower florets, steamed
- 2 cups cheddar cheese
- 1 cup milk
- 2 tbsp butter
- 2 tbsp flour
- Salt and pepper

Instructions:

1. Cook macaroni and steam cauliflower.
2. Make cheese sauce with butter, flour, milk, and cheddar.
3. Combine macaroni, cheese sauce, and cauliflower.
4. Bake at 350°F for 20 minutes.

Mac and Cheese with Sausage

Ingredients:

- 1 lb elbow macaroni
- 1 lb Italian sausage, casing removed
- 2 cups cheddar cheese
- 1 cup milk
- 2 tbsp butter
- 2 tbsp flour
- Salt and pepper

Instructions:

1. Cook macaroni.
2. Brown sausage in skillet and drain excess fat.
3. Prepare cheese sauce with butter, flour, milk, and cheddar.
4. Mix sausage, macaroni, and cheese sauce.
5. Bake at 350°F for 20 minutes.

Baked Mac and Cheese with Breadcrumbs

Ingredients:

- 1 lb elbow macaroni
- 3 cups cheddar cheese
- 2 cups milk
- 3 tbsp butter
- 3 tbsp flour
- 1 cup breadcrumbs
- 1 tbsp olive oil or melted butter
- Salt and pepper

Instructions:

1. Cook macaroni and drain.
2. Make cheese sauce: melt butter, whisk in flour, gradually add milk, cook until thickened, then stir in cheese.
3. Mix cheese sauce with macaroni, transfer to baking dish.
4. Toss breadcrumbs with olive oil or melted butter, sprinkle on top.
5. Bake at 350°F for 25-30 minutes until golden and bubbly.

Four Meat Mac and Cheese

Ingredients:

- 1 lb elbow macaroni
- 1/4 lb bacon, cooked and chopped
- 1/4 lb Italian sausage, cooked and crumbled
- 1/4 lb ham, diced
- 1/4 lb ground beef, cooked and drained
- 3 cups sharp cheddar cheese, shredded
- 2 cups milk
- 3 tbsp butter
- 3 tbsp flour
- Salt and pepper

Instructions:

1. Cook macaroni and drain.
2. Cook all meats separately until done.
3. Make cheese sauce: melt butter, whisk in flour, add milk gradually, cook until thickened, stir in cheese until melted.
4. Combine macaroni, meats, and cheese sauce.
5. Bake at 350°F for 20-25 minutes until bubbly.

Mac and Cheese with Roasted Red Peppers

Ingredients:

- 1 lb elbow macaroni
- 1 cup roasted red peppers, chopped
- 3 cups sharp cheddar cheese
- 2 cups milk
- 3 tbsp butter
- 3 tbsp flour
- Salt and pepper

Instructions:

1. Cook macaroni.
2. Prepare cheese sauce with butter, flour, milk, and cheddar.
3. Fold in chopped roasted red peppers.
4. Mix with macaroni and bake at 350°F for 20 minutes.

Mediterranean Mac and Cheese

Ingredients:

- 1 lb elbow macaroni
- 1 cup sun-dried tomatoes, chopped
- 1/2 cup Kalamata olives, sliced
- 1 cup feta cheese, crumbled
- 2 cups mozzarella cheese
- 2 cups milk
- 3 tbsp butter
- 3 tbsp flour
- 1 tsp dried oregano
- Salt and pepper

Instructions:

1. Cook macaroni.
2. Make cheese sauce with butter, flour, milk, mozzarella, and oregano.
3. Fold in sun-dried tomatoes, olives, and feta.
4. Combine with macaroni and bake at 350°F for 20 minutes.

Blue Cheese and Walnut Mac and Cheese

Ingredients:

- 1 lb elbow macaroni
- 1 1/2 cups sharp cheddar cheese
- 1/2 cup blue cheese, crumbled
- 1 cup milk
- 3 tbsp butter
- 3 tbsp flour
- 1/2 cup walnuts, toasted and chopped
- Salt and pepper

Instructions:

1. Cook macaroni.
2. Prepare cheese sauce with butter, flour, milk, and cheddar cheese.
3. Stir in blue cheese until melted.
4. Mix with macaroni and fold in walnuts.
5. Bake at 350°F for 20 minutes.

Truffle Oil and Mushroom Mac and Cheese

Ingredients:

- 1 lb elbow macaroni
- 2 cups mixed mushrooms, sliced
- 3 cups Gruyere or sharp white cheddar cheese
- 2 cups milk
- 3 tbsp butter
- 3 tbsp flour
- 1-2 tsp truffle oil (to taste)
- Salt and pepper

Instructions:

1. Cook macaroni.
2. Sauté mushrooms in butter until browned, set aside.
3. Make cheese sauce with butter, flour, milk, and cheese.
4. Stir in mushrooms and truffle oil.
5. Combine with macaroni and bake at 350°F for 20 minutes.

Mac and Cheese with Ham and Peas

Ingredients:

- 1 lb elbow macaroni
- 1 cup diced cooked ham
- 1 cup peas (fresh or frozen, thawed)
- 3 cups cheddar cheese
- 2 cups milk
- 3 tbsp butter
- 3 tbsp flour
- Salt and pepper

Instructions:

1. Cook macaroni.
2. Make cheese sauce with butter, flour, milk, and cheese.
3. Fold in ham and peas.
4. Mix with macaroni and bake at 350°F for 20 minutes.

BBQ Chicken Mac and Cheese

Ingredients:

- 1 lb elbow macaroni
- 2 cups cooked shredded chicken
- 1/2 cup BBQ sauce
- 3 cups cheddar cheese
- 2 cups milk
- 3 tbsp butter
- 3 tbsp flour
- Salt and pepper

Instructions:

1. Cook macaroni.
2. Make cheese sauce with butter, flour, milk, and cheddar.
3. Toss shredded chicken in BBQ sauce, fold into cheese sauce.
4. Mix with macaroni and bake at 350°F for 20 minutes.

Mac and Cheese with Spinach and Bacon

Ingredients:

- 1 lb elbow macaroni
- 4 slices bacon, cooked and chopped
- 2 cups fresh spinach, sautéed
- 3 cups cheddar cheese
- 2 cups milk
- 3 tbsp butter
- 3 tbsp flour
- Salt and pepper

Instructions:

1. Cook macaroni.
2. Sauté spinach until wilted, set aside.
3. Prepare cheese sauce with butter, flour, milk, and cheese.
4. Stir in bacon and spinach.
5. Combine with macaroni and bake at 350°F for 20 minutes.

Smoked Gouda Mac and Cheese

Ingredients:

- 1 lb elbow macaroni
- 3 cups smoked Gouda cheese, shredded
- 2 cups milk
- 3 tbsp butter
- 3 tbsp flour
- Salt and pepper

Instructions:

1. Cook macaroni, drain.
2. Melt butter, whisk in flour, gradually add milk and cook until thickened.
3. Stir in smoked Gouda until melted and smooth.
4. Combine with macaroni and bake at 350°F for 20 minutes or serve creamy.

Mac and Cheese with Roasted Garlic

Ingredients:

- 1 lb elbow macaroni
- 3 cups sharp cheddar cheese
- 2 cups milk
- 3 tbsp butter
- 3 tbsp flour
- 1 whole head roasted garlic, cloves mashed
- Salt and pepper

Instructions:

1. Roast garlic (wrap whole head in foil, roast at 400°F for 30-40 mins).
2. Cook macaroni.
3. Make cheese sauce and stir in roasted garlic.
4. Mix with pasta and bake or serve immediately.

Lobster and Spinach Mac and Cheese

Ingredients:

- 1 lb elbow macaroni
- 2 cups cooked lobster meat, chopped
- 2 cups fresh spinach, sautéed
- 3 cups white cheddar cheese
- 2 cups milk
- 3 tbsp butter
- 3 tbsp flour
- Salt and pepper

Instructions:

1. Cook macaroni.
2. Prepare cheese sauce with butter, flour, milk, and cheese.
3. Fold in lobster and spinach.
4. Combine with pasta and bake at 350°F for 20 minutes.

Mac and Cheese with Sundried Tomatoes

Ingredients:

- 1 lb elbow macaroni
- 1 cup sundried tomatoes, chopped
- 3 cups cheddar cheese
- 2 cups milk
- 3 tbsp butter
- 3 tbsp flour
- Salt and pepper

Instructions:

1. Cook macaroni.
2. Make cheese sauce and stir in sundried tomatoes.
3. Combine with pasta and bake at 350°F for 20 minutes.

Mac and Cheese with Chorizo

Ingredients:

- 1 lb elbow macaroni
- 1 cup chorizo, cooked and crumbled
- 3 cups sharp cheddar cheese
- 2 cups milk
- 3 tbsp butter
- 3 tbsp flour
- Salt and pepper

Instructions:

1. Cook macaroni.
2. Prepare cheese sauce.
3. Stir in cooked chorizo.
4. Mix with macaroni and bake at 350°F for 20 minutes.

Buffalo Ranch Mac and Cheese

Ingredients:

- 1 lb elbow macaroni
- 2 cups shredded cheddar cheese
- 1 cup shredded mozzarella
- 1/2 cup buffalo wing sauce
- 1/2 cup ranch dressing
- 2 cups milk
- 3 tbsp butter
- 3 tbsp flour
- Salt and pepper

Instructions:

1. Cook macaroni.
2. Make cheese sauce, stir in buffalo sauce and ranch dressing.
3. Add cheeses and combine with pasta.
4. Bake at 350°F for 20 minutes.

Mac and Cheese with Caramelized Shallots

Ingredients:

- 1 lb elbow macaroni
- 3 large shallots, thinly sliced
- 3 tbsp butter
- 3 cups sharp cheddar cheese
- 2 cups milk
- 3 tbsp flour
- Salt and pepper

Instructions:

1. Cook macaroni.
2. Caramelize shallots in butter over low heat until golden and soft (about 15-20 minutes).
3. Make cheese sauce and fold in caramelized shallots.
4. Combine with pasta and bake at 350°F for 20 minutes.

Mac and Cheese with Crispy Onions

Ingredients:

- 1 lb elbow macaroni
- 1 cup crispy fried onions (store-bought or homemade)
- 3 cups cheddar cheese
- 2 cups milk
- 3 tbsp butter
- 3 tbsp flour
- Salt and pepper

Instructions:

1. Cook macaroni.
2. Prepare cheese sauce.
3. Mix with pasta and half the crispy onions.
4. Top with remaining onions and bake at 350°F for 20 minutes.

Mac and Cheese with Roasted Brussels Sprouts

Ingredients:

- 1 lb elbow macaroni
- 2 cups Brussels sprouts, halved and roasted
- 3 cups sharp cheddar cheese
- 2 cups milk
- 3 tbsp butter
- 3 tbsp flour
- Salt and pepper

Instructions:

1. Roast Brussels sprouts at 400°F for 20-25 minutes until caramelized.
2. Cook macaroni.
3. Make cheese sauce and fold in Brussels sprouts.
4. Combine with pasta and bake at 350°F for 20 minutes.

Mac and Cheese with Ham and Mustard

Ingredients:

- 1 lb elbow macaroni
- 2 cups cooked ham, diced
- 3 cups sharp cheddar cheese
- 2 cups milk
- 3 tbsp butter
- 3 tbsp flour
- 2 tbsp Dijon mustard
- Salt and pepper

Instructions:

1. Cook macaroni, drain.
2. Melt butter, whisk in flour, slowly add milk, cook until thickened.
3. Stir in cheese until melted, then add Dijon mustard.
4. Fold in ham and combine with macaroni.
5. Bake at 350°F for 20 minutes if desired.

Mac and Cheese with Sriracha

Ingredients:

- 1 lb elbow macaroni
- 3 cups cheddar cheese
- 2 cups milk
- 3 tbsp butter
- 3 tbsp flour
- 2-3 tbsp sriracha (adjust to taste)
- Salt and pepper

Instructions:

1. Cook macaroni.
2. Make cheese sauce as usual, stir in sriracha.
3. Combine with pasta and bake or serve creamy.

Mac and Cheese with Prosciutto

Ingredients:

- 1 lb elbow macaroni
- 4 oz prosciutto, chopped and crisped
- 3 cups fontina or mozzarella cheese
- 2 cups milk
- 3 tbsp butter
- 3 tbsp flour
- Salt and pepper

Instructions:

1. Cook macaroni.
2. Prepare cheese sauce, stir in prosciutto pieces.
3. Mix with pasta and bake at 350°F for 20 minutes.

Mac and Cheese with Spinach and Artichokes

Ingredients:

- 1 lb elbow macaroni
- 2 cups fresh spinach, sautéed
- 1 cup marinated artichoke hearts, chopped
- 3 cups mozzarella and cheddar blend
- 2 cups milk
- 3 tbsp butter
- 3 tbsp flour
- Salt and pepper

Instructions:

1. Cook macaroni.
2. Make cheese sauce and fold in spinach and artichokes.
3. Mix with pasta and bake at 350°F for 20 minutes.

Mac and Cheese with Chives and Bacon

Ingredients:

- 1 lb elbow macaroni
- 6 slices cooked bacon, crumbled
- 1/4 cup fresh chives, chopped
- 3 cups sharp cheddar cheese
- 2 cups milk
- 3 tbsp butter
- 3 tbsp flour
- Salt and pepper

Instructions:

1. Cook macaroni.
2. Prepare cheese sauce.
3. Stir in bacon and chives, then combine with pasta.
4. Bake or serve creamy.

Mac and Cheese with Gorgonzola

Ingredients:

- 1 lb elbow macaroni
- 1 cup crumbled Gorgonzola cheese
- 2 cups sharp cheddar or Gruyère
- 2 cups milk
- 3 tbsp butter
- 3 tbsp flour
- Salt and pepper

Instructions:

1. Cook macaroni.
2. Make cheese sauce, stir in Gorgonzola and cheddar.
3. Combine with pasta and bake at 350°F for 20 minutes.

Mac and Cheese with Smoked Salmon

Ingredients:

- 1 lb elbow macaroni
- 6 oz smoked salmon, chopped
- 3 cups cream cheese and cheddar mix
- 2 cups milk
- 3 tbsp butter
- 3 tbsp flour
- 1 tbsp lemon juice
- Fresh dill (optional)
- Salt and pepper

Instructions:

1. Cook macaroni.
2. Prepare cheese sauce with cream cheese and cheddar, add lemon juice.
3. Fold in smoked salmon and dill.
4. Mix with pasta and serve immediately.

Mac and Cheese with Roasted Butternut Squash

Ingredients:

- 1 lb elbow macaroni
- 2 cups roasted butternut squash, mashed
- 3 cups sharp cheddar cheese
- 2 cups milk
- 3 tbsp butter
- 3 tbsp flour
- 1/2 tsp nutmeg
- Salt and pepper

Instructions:

1. Roast butternut squash until tender, mash.
2. Cook macaroni.
3. Make cheese sauce, stir in mashed squash and nutmeg.
4. Combine with pasta and bake at 350°F for 20 minutes.

Mac and Cheese with Pulled Beef

Ingredients:

- 1 lb elbow macaroni
- 2 cups pulled beef (slow-cooked or leftover)
- 3 cups cheddar cheese
- 2 cups milk
- 3 tbsp butter
- 3 tbsp flour
- BBQ sauce (optional)
- Salt and pepper

Instructions:

1. Cook macaroni.
2. Prepare cheese sauce.
3. Mix pulled beef into sauce, add a splash of BBQ sauce if desired.
4. Combine with pasta and bake at 350°F for 20 minutes.